Handy Indiana Genealogy Handbook

Gary L. Morris

ISBN-13: 978-1508415084

ISBN-10: 1508415080

Table of Contents

Notes

Genealogical Research in Indiana

From the early days of the wilderness explorers to modern times, Indiana has been known as the crossroads of America. Many of those passing through settled in the area, and as a result there are a wide variety of multi-cultural genealogical records available for the state. To get you started in tracing your Indiana ancestry, we'll introduce you to which of those records you'll need, and help you to understand:

1. What they are
2. Where to find them
3. How to use them

These records can be found both online and off, so we'll introduce you to online websites, indexes and databases, as well as brick-and-mortar repositories and other institutions that will help with your research in Indiana. So that you will have a more comprehensive understanding of these records, we have provided a brief history of the "Hoosier State" to illustrate what type of records may have been generated during specific time periods. That information will assist you in pinpointing times and locations on which to focus the search for your Indiana ancestors and their records.

A Brief History of Indiana

Indiana's earliest known settlers were the Native American mound builders, and it wasn't until the late 17th century that the first Europeans entered the area. Those early explorers were mainly French, and they discovered the region to be inhabited by the Delaware, Miami, and Potawatamie tribes. The first permanent settlement was established in 1732 at Vincennes, and the French controlled the area until 1763 when they ceded the land to Great Britain at the End of the French and Indian Wars.

With the implementation of the Quebec act in 1774, Indiana was united with Quebec, and at the end of the revolutionary War, the British ceded Indiana and the rest of the Old Northwest to the United States. Indiana became a part of the Northwest Territory when it was established in 1787, and the area at that time was still largely unsettled. Native Americans resisted any settlement by white Europeans, though that resistance was eventually ended at the Battle of Tippecanoe in 1811.

The Indiana territory was established in 1800, and included the states of Indiana, Wisconsin, and Illinois as well as parts of Minnesota and Michigan. The original capital was Vincennes, but was moved to Corydon in 1813. Indiana achieved statehood in 1816, and Indianapolis was made capital in 1824-1825. The Wabash and Erie Canal opened in the 1840's giving Indiana a link to eastern markets via Lake Erie. In the same time period the first railroad to Indiana opened, and the modern era began.

Indiana experienced many changes during the Civil War era, the state voting for Abraham Lincoln, and supporting the Union cause. There was one Confederate raid into Indiana during the Civil War, but otherwise the state saw little action except for that of its troops sent to the southern arena.

Important Dates in Indiana History

1679 - Claimed by France
1732 - Vincennes founded
1763 - Ceded by French to Great Britain
1784 – Clarksville founded
1787 – Becomes part of Northwest
1800 – Territory of Indiana created
1811 – Native American tribes defeated at the Battle of Tippecanoe
1814 – Organized as separate territory
1816 – Statehood
1839 – Regular railroad service begins

Famous Battles Fought in Indiana

Several military confrontations have occurred within the boundaries of what is modern-day Indiana. Many took place during **The French and Indian War** between 1754 and 1763. Many other skirmished occurred during the War of 1812, and battle accounts as well as service and genealogical records for soldiers who fought during those battles can be found at **The Society of the War of 1812 in the State of Indiana.**

The battle accounts can be very effective in uncovering the military records of your ancestor. They can tell you what regiments fought in which battles, and often include the names and ranks of many officers and enlisted men.

The French and Indian Waro:
http://www.kidport.com/reflib/usahistory/frenchindian/frenindwar.htm

The Society of the War of 1812 in the State of Indiana:
http://lineage.gradeless.com/Indiana_1812.htm

Common Indiana Genealogical Issues and Resources to Overcome Them

Boundary Changes: Boundary changes are a common obstacle when researching Indiana ancestors. You could be searching for an ancestor's record in one county when in fact it is stored in a different one due to historical county boundary changes. The **Atlas of Historical County Boundaries** can help you to overcome that problem. It provides a chronological listing of every boundary change that has occurred in the history of Indiana.

Atlas of Historical County Boundaries:
http://publications.newberry.org/ahcbp/documents/IN_Consolidated
_Chronology.htm#Consolidated_Chronology

Name Changes: Surname changes, variations, and misspellings can complicate genealogical research. It is important to check all spelling variations. Soundex, a program that indexes names by sound, is a useful first step, but you can't rely on it completely as some name variations result in different Soundex codes. The surnames could be different, but the first name may be different too. You can also find records filed under initials, middle names, and nicknames as well, so you will need to **get creative with surname variations** and spellings in order to cover all the possibilities. For help with surname variations read our instructional article on **How to Use Soundex**.

get creative with surname variations:
http://obituarieshelp.org/blog/?p=634

How to Use Soundex: http://obituarieshelp.org/blog/?p=505

Indiana Genealogical Organizations and Archives

Genealogical resources include not only records, but the organizations that house them, or can direct you to them. These institutions include: *Archives, Libraries, Genealogical Societies, Family History Centers, Universities, Churches, and Museums.*

Following are links to their websites, their physical addresses, and a summary of the records you can find there.

Indiana Archives

Indiana State Archives – military records, county and Supreme court records, orphanage records,

6440 E. 30th St.
Indianapolis, Indiana 46219
Phone: (317) 591-5222

Indiana State Archives: http://www.in.gov/icpr/3017.htm

Indiana State Library, Genealogy Collection - family histories, indexes to records, cemetery transcriptions, microfilmed federal census records, county records, passenger lists, and military pension data

140 N. Senate Avenue
Indianapolis, Indiana 46204
Phone: (317) 232-3675

Indiana State Library, Genealogy Collection:
http://www.in.gov/library/genealogy.htm

National Archives Great Lakes Region (Chicago) - federal censuses, passenger lists, naturalization indexes, General Land Office records for Indiana 1808–1876 ,Indian census rolls 1885–1940, records of marine inspection and navigation for Indiana ,1865–1968 including names of vessel owners, masters, and crew members, U.S. District and Circuit Court records for Indiana 1819 – 1961, various military records

7358 South Pulaski Road
Chicago, IL 60629
Telephone: 773-948-9001
Fax: 773-948-9050

National Archives Great Lakes Region (Chicago):
http://www.archives.gov/chicago/

Allen County Public Library Genealogy Center - databases of county and state, records as well as African-American, military, and Bible records. Some of the center's resources have been digitized and can be searched online at **Brigham Young University's Harold B. Lee Library Digital Collections**.

Allen County Public Library
900 Library Plaza
Fort Wayne, IN 46802
Phone: 260.421.1225
Fax: 260.421.1386

Allen County Public Library Genealogy Center:
http://www.genealogycenter.org/Databases.aspx

Brigham Young University's Harold B. Lee Library Digital Collections: http://contentdm.lib.byu.edu/cdm/search/cosuppress/

Indiana Genealogical and Historical Societies

Genealogical and historical societies have access to extensive catalogues of genealogical data. They are also able to offer expert guidance for genealogical researchers. Many members are professional genealogists who are most willing to share their expertise in finding ancestors.

Indiana Genealogical Society - more than 500,000 records representing all of Indiana's ninety two counties

P.O. Box 10507
Fort Wayne, IN 46825-0507

Indiana Genealogical Society: www.indgensoc.org

Indiana Historical Society – manuscripts, oral histories, business collections, historical photographs (digitized),

315 West Ohio Street
Indianapolis, IN 46202
Telephone: 317-232-1882
Fax: 317-233-3109

Indiana Historical Society: http://www.indianahistory.org/our-collections

Indiana Family History Centers

The Family History Centers run by the LDS Church offer free access to billions of genealogical records for free to the general public. They also provide classes on genealogy and one-on-one assistance to inexperienced family historians. Here you will find a **Complete Listing of Indiana Family History Centers**.

Complete Listing of Indiana Family History Centers: https://familysearch.org/locations/centerlocator

Additional Indiana Genealogical Resources

Indiana Mailing Lists

Mailing lists are internet based facilities that use email to distribute a single message to all who subscribe to it. When information on a particular surname, new records, or any other important genealogy information related to the mailing list topic becomes available, the subscribers are alerted to it. Joining a mailing list is an excellent way to stay up to date on Indiana genealogy research topics. Rootsweb have an extensive listing of **Indiana Mailing Lists** on a variety of topics.

Indiana Mailing Lists:
http://lists.rootsweb.ancestry.com/index/usa/IN/misc.html

Indiana Message Boards

A message board is another internet based facility where people can post questions about a specific genealogy topic and have it answered by other genealogists. If you have questions about a surname, record type, or research topic, you can post your question and other researchers and genealogists will help you with the answer. Be sure to check back regularly, as the answers are not emailed to you. The Indiana message boards at **Rootsweb** are completely free to use.

Rootsweb:
http://boards.rootsweb.com/localities.northam.usa.states/mb.ashx

Indiana Newspapers and Periodicals

Many genealogy periodicals and historical newspapers contain reprinted copies of family genealogies, transcripts of family Bible records, information about local records and archives, census indexes, church records, queries, land records, obituaries, court records, cemetery records, and wills. The following sites have historical Indiana newspapers and periodicals that you can search online or on-site.

Indiana Historic Newspaper Digitization Project – ongoing project of digitizing 19th century Indiana newspapers

Indiana Historic Newspaper Digitization Project: http://indiananewspapers.wordpress.com/

Indiana Historical Society - more than 1,200 titles comprising of over 9 million pages of Indiana newspapers

Indiana Historical Society : http://www.indianahistory.org/our-services/conservation/indiana-newspapers-on-microfilm

GenealogyBank.com – free searchable database of Indiana newspaper archives, 1817-1975

GenealogyBank.com: http://www.genealogybank.com/gbnk/newspapers/explore/USA/Indiana/

Library of Congress Digital Newspaper Directory – free searchable database of historical U.S. newspapers dating from 1690-present

Library of Congress Digital Newspaper Directory: http://chroniclingamerica.loc.gov/search/titles/

The Online Books Page – links to historical books and periodicals available for viewing online, dating from mid-16th century

The Online Books Pageo: http://onlinebooks.library.upenn.edu

NewspaperArchive.com – largest online database of historical newspapers in the world.

NewspaperArchive.com: http://newspaperarchive.com/

Historical Indiana Maps and Gazetteers

Maps are an integral part of genealogical research. They help us to locate landmarks, towns, cities, parishes, states, provinces, waterways and roads and streets. They also help us to determine when and where boundary changes might have taken place, and give us a visualization of the area we're researching in.

For locating place names, a gazetteer is the best possible resource for any genealogist. Gazetteers are also sometimes called "place name dictionaries", and can help you to locate the area in which you need to conduct research. Below are links to the maps and gazetteers for research in Indiana.

Peabody GNIS Service – Indiana:
http://peabody.research.yale.edu/cgi-bin/Query.GNIS?ST=Indiana&SU=1

Color Landform Atlas – Indiana:
http://fermi.jhuapl.edu/states/in_0.html

1985 U.S. Atlas: http://www.livgenmi.com/1895/IN/

Indiana Hometown Locator: http://indiana.hometownlocator.com/

Indiana City Directories

.

City directories are similar to telephone directories in that they list the residents of a particular area. The difference though is what is important to genealogists, and that is they pre-date telephone directories. You can find an ancestor's information such as their street address, place of employment, occupation, or the name of their spouse. A one-stop-shop for finding city directories in Indiana is the **Indiana Online Historical Directories** which contains a listing of every available historical directory related to Indiana.

Indiana Online Historical Directories:
https://sites.google.com/site/onlinedirectorysite/Home/usa/in

Indianapolis City Directory Collection, Indiana University - Large database of individual city and county directories that can be viewed online

Indianapolis City Directory Collection, Indiana University:
http://indiamond6.ulib.iupui.edu/cdm/search/collection/ICD

Indiana City Directories at DistantCousin - free online archive of Indiana city directory records and scanned images that can be searched and viewed online

Indiana City Directories at DistantCousin:
http://distantcousin.com/Directories/IN/

Indiana Genealogical Records

Birth, Death, Marriage and Divorce Records – Also known as vital records, birth, death, and marriage certificates are the most basic, yet most important records attached to your ancestor. The reason for their importance is that they not only place your ancestor in a specific place at a definite time, but potentially connect the individual to other relatives. Below is a list of repositories and websites where you can find Indiana vital records

Birth and death records were not required in Indiana until 1882. Birth records for individuals born between 1882 and 1906 can be found at the individual **County Health Office** where the birth occurred.

County Health Office: http://www.in.gov/isdh/20422.htm

For birth records from 1907 and death records after 1900, researchers must order copies from:

Indiana State Department of Health
2 North Meridian Street
Indianapolis, IN 46204
(317) 233-1325

Indiana State Department of Health:
http://www.in.gov/isdh/20444.htm

Indiana State Library – marriage indexes pre 1850, 1957-1992, and 1993 – 2004, WPA birth and death indexes

Indiana State Library: http://www.in.gov/library/

Individual **Clerks of the Circuit Court** maintain divorce records form 1852 and applications may be made in writing.

Clerks of the Circuit Court: http://www.in.gov/icpr/2502.htm

Family Search has the following indexes which can be searched online:

- **Indiana, Births and Christenings, 1773-1933**
- **Indiana, Marriages, 1811-1959**
- **Indiana, Marriages, 1780-1992**
- **Indiana, Death Index, 1882-1920**

Indiana, Births and Christenings, 1773-1933:
https://familysearch.org/search/collection/1674814

Indiana, Marriages, 1811-1959:
https://familysearch.org/search/collection/1410397

Indiana, Marriages, 1780-1992:
https://familysearch.org/search/collection/1674830

Indiana, Death Index, 1882-1920:
https://familysearch.org/search/collection/1947977

Census Reports

Census records are among the most important genealogical documents for placing your ancestor in a particular place at a specific time. Like BDM records, they can also lead you to other ancestors, particularly those who were living under the authority of the head of household.

Federal census records for Indiana exist from 1829 to 1990, and there is a partial territorial census for 1807. These reports can be found in the following repositories:

National Archives Great Lakes Region (Chicago) - federal censuses and Indian census rolls

7358 South Pulaski Road
Chicago, IL 60629
Telephone: 773-948-9001
Fax: 773-948-9050

National Archives Great Lakes Region (Chicago):
http://www.archives.gov/chicago/

U.S. National Archives – Federal censuses form 1790-1930

U.S. National Archives : http://www.archives.gov/research/census/

The **Free Census Project** has transcribed many Indiana indexes and new material is added daily

Free Census Project : http://usgwcensus.org/cenfiles/in.htm

Access Genealogy - Indiana census records from 1820-1930

Access Genealogy:
http://www.accessgenealogy.com/census/indiana-census-records.htm

African American Census Schedules Online – slave schedules, mortality schedules, slave-owners census

African American Census Schedules Online:
http://www.afrigeneas.com/aacensus/

Native Americans in Census Records (US National Archives)

Native Americans in Census Records:
http://www.archives.gov/research/census/native-americans/

Indiana Church Records

Church and synagogue records are a valuable resource, especially for baptisms, marriages, and burials that took place before 1900. You will need to at least have an idea of your ancestor's religious denomination, and in most cases you will have to visit a brick and mortar establishment to view them.

Most church records are kept by the individual church, although in some denominations, records are placed in a regional archive or maintained at the diocesan level. Local Historical Societies are sometimes the repository for the state's older church records. Below are links archives that maintain church records, as well as a few databases that can be viewed online.

The **Family History Library** contains many church records from a variety of denominations on microfilm.

Family History Library:
http://familysearch.org/learn/wiki/en/Family_History_Library

The **Swenson Center** at Augustana College in Rock Island Illinois has a collection of Lutheran, Evangelical, and Baptist records for Indiana.
Swenson Center: http://www.augustana.edu/general-information/swenson-center-/genealogy/church-records/idaho---indiana

Allen County Public Library Genealogy Center in Fort Wayne has a large collection of multi-denominational records from around the state.
Allen County Public Library
900 Library Plaza
Fort Wayne, IN 46802
Phone: 260.421.1225
Fax: 260.421.1386

Allen County Public Library Genealogy Center:
http://www.genealogycenter.org/pdf/AllenCountyINCongregations.pdf

The Indiana State Library has a huge collection of religious records for specific churches, parishes, counties, and towns which include Mennonite, Huguenot, Quaker, Lutheran, Baptist, Jewish, Methodist, Roman Catholic, Anglican, Episcopalian, Mormon, and Presbyterian records

Central Repositories for Denominational Records

Most of the records of individual denominations are kept in central repositories. Below is a list of the major congregational archives for Indiana with links to their websites, physical addresses, and contact information.

Baptist

Indiana Baptist Collection
Franklin College Library
101 Branigin Blvd
Franklin, IN 46131-2623
Phone: (317) 738-8162 or 1-(800) 852-0232
Fax: (317) 738-8787
Email: library@franklincollege.edu

Franklin College Library: http://www.franklincollege.edu/

Church of Jesus Christ of Latter-day Saints (Mormons)

Early Mormon church records for Indiana can be found on microfilm at the LDS Family History Library in Salt Lake City; film numbers can be located through the **Family History Library Catalog** .

Family History Library Catalog:
https://familysearch.org/eng/Library/FHLC/frameset_fhlc.asp

Lutheran

Archives of the Evangelical Lutheran Church in America
321 Bonnie Lane,
Elk Grove Village, IL 60007

Alternate mailing address:
8765 W. Higgins Rd.
Chicago, IL 60631
Phone: (847) 690-9410
Fax: (847) 690-9502
E-mail: archives@elca.org

Archives of the Evangelical Lutheran Church in America:
http://www.elca.org/Who-We-Are/History/ELCA-Archives.aspx

Methodist

Archives of DePauw University and Indiana United Methodism
Roy O. West Library
11 E Larabee St
P.O. Box 37
Greencastle, IN 46135-0037
Phone: (765) 658-4406
Fax: (765) 658-4423
E-mail: archives@depauw.edu

Archives of DePauw University and Indiana United Methodism
link to:
http://www.depauw.edu/libraries/about/librarylocations/archives/

Moravian

The Moravian Archives
41 West Locust Street
Bethlehem, Pennsylvania 18018
United States of America
Phone: (610) 866-3255
Fax: (610) 866-9210

The Moravian Archives:
http://www.moravianchurcharchives.org/general.php

Presbyterian

Archives of the Presbyterian Church of Indiana
Duggan Library
P.O. Box 287
Hanover, IN 47243-0287
Phone: (812) 866-7165
Fax: (812) 866-7172

Archives of the Presbyterian Church of Indiana:
http://library.hanover.edu/archives/presbyterian.php

Roman Catholic

University of Notre Dame Archives
607 Hesburgh Library
Notre Dame, IN 46556
Phone: (574) 631-6448
Fax: (574) 631-7980
E-mail: **archives@nd.edu**

University of Notre Dame Archives: http://archives.nd.edu/

The records of all four Indiana Roman Catholic dioceses and the early church records of Vincennes (Knox County) are available on microfilm at the **Family History Library**.

Family History Library:
https://familysearch.org/learn/wiki/en/Family_History_Library

Diocese of Evansville
4200 N. Kentucky Ave.
P.O. Box 4169
Evansville, IN 47724-0169
Phone: (812) 424-5536

Diocese of Evansville: http://www.evansville-diocese.org/

Diocese of Fort Wayne-South Bend
Archbishop Noll Catholic Center,
915 South Clinton
P.O. Box 390
Fort Wayne, IN 46801
Phone: (260) 422-4611

Diocese of Fort Wayne-South Bend:
http://www.diocesefwsb.org/Diocesan-Archives

Diocese of Gary
9292 Broadway
Merrillville, IN 46410
Phone: (219) 769-9292

Diocese of Gary: http://www.dcgary.org/

Archdiocese of Indianapolis
1400 N. Meridian Street
Indianapolis, IN 46202
Phone: (800) 382-9836

Archdiocese of Indianapolis:
http://www.archindy.org/archives/index.html

Diocese of Lafayette
P.O. Box 260
Lafayette, IN 47902-0260
Phone: (765) 742-4852

Diocese of Lafayette: http://www.dol-in.org/

Indiana Military Records

More than 40 million Americans have participated in some time of war service since America was colonized. The chance of finding your ancestor amongst those records is exceptionally high. Military records can even reveal individuals who never actually served, such as those who registered for the two World Wars but were never called to duty.

Below are a number of links to websites and archives that contain Indiana military records.

Indiana State Archives – military records from the Black Hawk War, Civil War, Mexican War, and the National Guard

6440 E. 30th St.
Indianapolis, Indiana 46219
Phone: (317) 591-5222

Indiana State Archives: http://www.in.gov/icpr/3017.htm

Indiana Genealogical Society – large collection of Civil War records that includes burials, unit rosters, and casualties

P.O. Box 10507
Fort Wayne, IN 46825-0507

Indiana Genealogical Society: www.indgensoc.org

U.S. National Archives – WWI Draft registration cards, casualties lists, WWI and WWII service records, Korean War records, Vietnam War records, Civil War and Spanish-American War records, and casualties lists.

U.S. National Archives:
http://www.archives.gov/research/military/veterans/online.html

US Department of Veterans Affairs Nationwide Gravesite Locator – includes information on veterans and their family members buried in veterans and military cemeteries having a government grave marker.

US Department of Veterans Affairs Nationwide Gravesite Locator: http://gravelocator.cem.va.gov/

United States Index to Indian Wars Pension Files, 1892-1926 – military pension records of soldiers who fought in the Indian Wars between 1817 and 1898

United States Index to Indian Wars Pension Files, 1892-1926: https://familysearch.org/search/collection/1979427

United States Registers of Enlistments in the U.S. Army, 1798-1914 - index of men who enlisted in the United States Army, 1798-1914.

United States Registers of Enlistments in the U.S. Army, 1798-1914: https://familysearch.org/search/collection/1880762

United States Mexican War Pension Index, 1887-1926 - index to Mexican War pension files for service between 1846 and 1848

United States Mexican War Pension Index, 1887-1926: https://familysearch.org/search/collection/1979390

Civil War Soldiers Service Records - Service records for both Union and Confederate soldiers indexed by soldier's name, rank, and unit.

Civil War Soldier Service Records: http://go.fold3.com/civilwar_records/

Indiana Cemetery Records

As convenient as it is to search cemetery records online, keep in mind that there are a few disadvantages over visiting a cemetery in person. They are:

- Tombstone information is not always accurately transcribed
- The arrangement of the graves in a cemetery can be crucial as family members are often buried next to each other or in the same grave. This arrangement is not always preserved in the alphabetical indexes that are found online.

With that information in mind, the following websites have databases that can be searched online for Indiana Cemetery records.

Indiana Tombstone Transcription Project - death and burial records

Indiana Tombstone Transcription Project:
http://www.usgwtombstones.org/indiana/indiana.html

Indiana State Library, Genealogy Collection – tombstone transcriptions

140 N. Senate Avenue
Indianapolis, Indiana 46204
Phone: (317) 232-3675

Indiana State Library, Genealogy Collection: http://www.in.gov/library/genealogy.htm

African American Cemeteries Online – African American, slave, and Native American cemetery records

African American Cemeteries Online:
http://africanamericancemeteries.com/

Access Genealogy – huge database of Indiana cemetery record transcriptions

Access Genealogy:
http://www.accessgenealogy.com/cemetery/indiana-cemetery-records.htm

Find a Grave – over 100 million grave records can be searched on this site. Search can be conducted by name, location, or cemetery name.

Find a Grave: http://www.findagrave.com/

Interment.net - A free online database containing approximately 4 million cemetery records from around the world.

Interment.net: http://www.interment.net/

Billion Graves – as the name implies, you can search a billion records including headstone photos, transcriptions, cemetery records, and grave locations.

Billion Graves:
http://billiongraves.com/pages/search/index.php#cemetery

Indiana Obituaries

Obituaries can reveal a wealth about our ancestor and other relatives. You can search our **Indiana Newspaper Obituaries Listings** from hundreds of Indiana newspapers online for free.

Indiana Newspaper Obituaries Listings:
http://obituarieshelp.org/indiana_newspaper_obituaries.html

Indiana Wills and Probate Records

The documents found in a probate packet may include a complete inventory of a person's estate, newspaper entries, witness testimony, a copy of a will, list of debtors and creditors, names of executors or trustees, names of heirs. They can not only tell you about the ancestor you're currently researching, but lead to other ancestors. Most of these records must be accessed at a county court or clerk's office, but some can be found online as well. You can obtain copies of the original probate records by writing to the county clerk.

Indiana probate records exist since 1790. They can be found at individual **Indiana Clerks of the County Court**

Indiana Clerks of the County Court:
http://www.in.gov/icpr/2502.htm

The Family History Library has microfilmed Probate Complete Order Books and Probate Order Books more than half the counties in Indiana. They can be searched for in the **Family History Library Catalogue**.

Family History Library Catalogue:
https://familysearch.org/eng/Library/FHLC/frameset_fhlc.asp

Indiana Immigration and Naturalization Records

The naturalization process generated many types of records, including petitions, declarations of intention, and oaths of allegiance. These records can provide family historians with information such as a person's birth date and place of birth, immigration year, marital status, spouse information, occupation, witnesses' names and addresses, and more.

Indiana State Archives – An Index to Naturalization Records Prior to 1907

6440 E. 30th St.
Indianapolis, Indiana 46219
Phone: (317) 591-5222

Indiana State Archives : http://www.in.gov/serv/icpr_naturalization

US National Archives – Immigration and Naturalization records for the entire United States

US National Archives:
http://www.archives.gov/research/immigration/passenger-arrival.html

Family Search has a searchable online index, the **Indiana Naturalization Records and Indexes, 1848-1992**

Indiana Naturalization Records and Indexes, 1848-1992:
https://familysearch.org/search/collection/2137708

Indiana Native American Records

Indiana State Library, Genealogy Collection – miscellaneous Native American resources including manuscripts, federal publications, histories, and biographies

140 N. Senate Avenue
Indianapolis, Indiana 46204
Phone: (317) 232-3675

Indiana State Library, Genealogy Collection link to: http://www.in.gov/library/genealogy.htm

Access Genealogy – Indiana Native American census records, tribal histories, and much more

Access Genealogy:
http://www.accessgenealogy.com/native/indiana-indian-tribes.htm

U.S. National Archives - information on American Indians who maintained their ties to Federally-recognized Tribes (1830-1970).

U.S. National Archives: http://www.archives.gov/research/native-americans/

Records of the Bureau of Indian Affairs (BIA) link to:
http://www.archives.gov/research/guide-fed-records/groups/075.html

Missing Matriarchs – Resources for Researching Female Indiana Ancestors

Looking for female ancestors requires an adjustment of how we view traditional records sources. A woman's identity was often under that of her husband, and often individual records for them can be difficult to locate. The following resources are effective in locating female ancestors in Indiana where traditional records may not reveal them.

Marriage and Divorce Records

The earliest marriages were recorded in the Parish registers of the Catholic Church, starting in 1749. The following records are available on microfilm:

- Saint Nicholas Xavier de Oubache parish registers, 1749-1786, (film 1026606) at the **French National Archives** in Paris, and transcripts at the **National Archives of Canada** in Ottawa, and parish registers, 1780-1960 (film 1433361 ff.) at **Saint Francis Xavier Church** in Vincennes.

County clerks have recorded marriages since around 1817, and state-wide registration commenced in 1958. The state legislature granted the first divorces from 1817-1851. Since 1852, county courts of common pleas have held jurisdiction over divorce.

The Indiana State Library has a database of **Marriages through 1850** extracted from county records and **Indiana Marriages 1958-2004**.

Marriages through 1850:
http://web.isl.lib.in.us/inmarriages1850/marriages_search.asp

Indiana Marriages 1958-2004:
http://web.isl.lib.in.us/indianamarriages/IN_marriages_search.asp

Bibliographies

1. *The Divorce Issue and Reform in Nineteenth Century Indiana*, Richard Wires (Ball State University Press, 1967)
2. *Women's History Collections Bibliography*, Indiana Historical Society Library
3. *When the Truth is Told: A History of Black Women's Culture and Community in Indiana, 1875-1950,* Council of Negro Women
4. *Pioneer Women of Lake County, Indiana 1834-1850,* Avis Bryant Brown and Ethel Alice Vinnege, (The Authors, 1979)

Selected Resources for Indiana Women's History

Lewis Historical Library
Vincennes University
Vincennes, IN 47951

Allen County Public Library
900 Webster St.
Box 2270
Fort Wayne, IN 46801

Common Indiana Surnames

The following surnames are among the most common in Indiana and are also being currently researched by other genealogists. If you find your surname here, there is a chance that some research has already been performed on your ancestor.

Abell, Adams, Albin, Allen, Allmon, Allstatt, Anderson, Apple, Ash, Ashworth Askren, Ayers, Bain, Baker, Bales, Barbre, Barger, Barr, Bates, Beach, Beatty, Beauchamp, Belcher, Bell, Bennington, Berry, Bishop, Bledsoe, Blunk, Bogue, Bolen, Bolling, Boyd, Branson, Brown, Brubech, Burlison, Burress, Busick, Carroll, Case, Chatham, Coffin, Condry, Conn, Conrad, Cook, Cope, Courtney, Cox, Crecelius, Crum, Curry, Cuzzort, De Witt, Denbo, Denney, Dickerson, Dillard, Dillon, Drake, Driskell, Duckworth, Eastridge, Enlow, Epler, Fee, Femin, Ferguson, Fields, Flick, Ford, Fuller, Gard, Gass, Gilliatt, Glenn, Goldman, Gregory, Grimes, Grose, Groves, Hammond, Hammonds, Harmon, Harris, Harrison, Haskins, Hatfield, Hawhee, Hoag, Hobbs, Hobson, Hollen, Humphrey, Hunt, James, Johnson, Kellams, Kendall, Keysacker, Kimmel, King, Knight, Land, Lane, Laswell, Lawrence, Leakey, Leatherburry, Leonard, Lett, Livingston, Lockridge, Lowe, Luttrell, Macy, Maloy, Marlett, Martin, Mason, Matthew, Mauck Maxwell, McCarty, McDonald, McIlvain, McIver, McQueen, McWilliams, Meredith, Messick, Mills, Miner, Mize, Morgan, Morin, Nation, Neal, Newbold, Newkirk, Newton, Pace, Palen, Palmer, Parks, Parsons, Patton, Paul, Polen, Polk, Price, Quick, Rankin, Renshaw, Rice, Riley, Roberts, Rogers, Scott, Searbrought, Sexton, Seybold, Sibens, Sinclair, Smith, Spears, Speedy, Spencer, Spicer, Stapp, Stephens, Stockinger, Stovall, Stroud, Sturm, Swayze, Taylor, Teaford, Thacker, Thatcher, Thompson, Thrash, Thurston, Trusty, Tucker, Underhill, Van Buskirk, Van Dorin, Van Winkle, Vernette, Walls, Weaver, White, Wilbur, Wiles, Wilkins, Williams, Wilson, , Woods, Wright, York

Notes

Notes

www.ingramcontent.com/pod-product-compliance
Lightning Source LLC
Chambersburg PA
CBHW071343310526
45790CB00018B/1244